CELEBRATING HALLOWEEN

BY ANN HEINRICHS • ILLUSTRATED BY TERI WEIDNER

Published by The Child's World®
1980 Lookout Drive • Mankato, MN 56003-1705
800-599-READ • www.childsworld.com

Copyright © 2022 by The Child's World®
All rights reserved. No part of this book may be reproduced or utilized in any form or by any means without written permission from the publisher.

ISBN 9781503853843 (Reinforced Library Binding)
ISBN 9781503854666 (Portable Document Format)
ISBN 9781503855045 (Online Multi-user eBook)
LCCN: 2021953050

Printed in the United States of America

ABOUT THE AUTHOR
Ann Heinrichs lives in Chicago, Illinois. She has written more than two hundred books for children. She loves traveling to faraway places.

ABOUT THE ILLUSTRATOR
Teri Weidner illustrated this spooky book using pastels and colored pencils. She lives with her husband Chris and their son Nicholas in Portsmouth, New Hampshire.

CONTENTS

Chapter 1	Trick or Treat!	4
Chapter 2	A Scary Night	6
Chapter 3	Roman Festivals	8
Chapter 4	All Hallows' Eve	10
Chapter 5	Costumes, Mischief, Apples, and Fun	12
Chapter 6	Begging for Treats	16
Chapter 7	The Jack-o'-Lantern	18
Chapter 8	The Day of the Dead	20
Chapter 9	Poetry Corner	22

Joining in the Spirit of Halloween 26
Making Spooky Spiders 28
Making Egg Carton Spiders 29
Glossary 30
Learn More 31
Index 32

CHAPTER 1
Trick or Treat!

Witches and ghosts dangle in windows. Black cats lurk in the bushes. Jack-o'-lanterns glow with toothy grins. Boo! It's Halloween!

Kids in costumes run giggling down the street. They ring their neighbors' doorbells. What a sight they are as they shout "Trick or Treat!"

> Hey-ho for Hallowe'en,
> When all the witches
> are to be seen;
> Some in black
> and some in green—
> Hey-ho for Hallowe'en!
> —Old British rhyme

Costumes, pumpkins, and candy are all part of the excitement of Halloween.

CHAPTER 2
A Scary Night

How did we get Halloween? It's a long story! It began with the **ancient** Celtic people. They once lived in Great Britain and Ireland.

November 1 was the Celtic New Year. The night before, Celts held a festival. It was called *Samhain* (SOW-en).

Celts believed the spirits of the dead rose up that night. They roamed around, causing trouble. How could people scare them off? By wearing costumes!

People tried to look as scary as could be. Some even wore animal heads. They made lots of noise, too. They had to scare those spirits away!

For the New Year, the Celts lit bonfires, or huge, open-air fires. The bonfires blazed on hilltops. They believed this would help scare the bad spirits away. The Celts also left food on their doorsteps for good spirits.

For Celts, Samhain was a time to scare spirits away.

CHAPTER 3
Roman Festivals

Many other ancient people held fall festivals. Fall was the time to gather crops. People celebrated their **harvests**.

Ancient fall festivals were a celebration of harvesttime.

Some ancient harvest festivals took place during the harvest moon. That's the full moon that rises in September. This marks the first day of autumn.

Pomona's name comes from a Latin word for fruit.

Ancient Romans held Feralia in October. This was a time to honor the dead. Another Roman festival honored Pomona. She was the **goddess** of fruit and trees. Her **symbol** was the apple.

The Romans took over Celtic lands. They joined their fall festivals with Samhain. Then everyone's customs got jumbled together!

Ancient Romans had another fall harvest festival called *Cerelia* (suh-RAY-lee-uh). Cerelia honored Ceres (SIHR-eez). She was the goddess of crops, especially grains. Our word "cereal" comes from "Ceres."

CHAPTER 4
All Hallows' Eve

In time, Christian beliefs spread through Europe. Old beliefs died out. But people still liked their **traditional** fall festivals.

Christian leaders used this. They simply changed the festivals' meanings. They made November 1 All Saints' Day. It was also called All Hallows' Day. Something hallowed is considered holy. All Hallows' Day was meant to honor the Christian saints.

The night before was October 31. That was All Hallows' Eve. Some people called it All Hallows' Evening or E'en. And that became the word *Halloween*!

The Christian Church declared November 1 All Saints' Day in about the year 837.

Christian beliefs eventually replaced the meaning behind ancient fall festivals.

CHAPTER 5

Costumes, Mischief, Apples, and Fun

Irish and British people eventually became Christians. Still, they kept some old customs. October 31 might be All Hallows' Eve. But it was still a scary night. That's when spirits roamed around.

People dressed as witches and ghosts. And they caused lots of **mischief**. It all helped scare the spirits away.

In some parts of Ireland, Halloween is called Pooky Night. It's named after a fairy called the pookah. Pookahs were said to be full of mischief!

Bobbing for apples is a tasty and challenging Halloween tradition!

Nut Crack Night

Early English settlers called Halloween "Nut Crack Night." That night, they tossed nuts into an open fire. Everyone watched how the nutshells glowed, burned, or burst. That gave clues about how things would go with one's sweetheart.

Apples were also part of Halloween. They recalled the Roman goddess Pomona. Bobbing for apples became a Halloween game. People floated apples in a tub of water. Then they tried to grab the apples with their teeth. Candy-coated apples became Halloween treats, too.

Candy apples have a crunchy coating. Caramel apples' coating is softer and stickier.

Witches, bats, and black cats all help to make Halloween spooky!

Immigrants brought their Halloween customs to the United States. These customs lost their old meanings over time. They simply became ways to have fun. Halloween continued to be a night for scary things. Like what? Witches, skeletons, black cats, spiders, and bats!

Black Cats

In some places, black cats are a sign of good luck. Fishermen's wives in Yorkshire, England, used to keep a black cat at home when their husbands went to sea. This was said to ensure their safe return.

CHAPTER 6

Begging for Treats

November 2 became a Christian holiday, too. It was named All Souls' Day. That was a day to honor the dead.

Christians in Europe went "souling" that day. They traveled from village to village, knocking on doors. At each house, they begged a different family for soul cakes. Those were little squares of bread with berries inside. The beggars made promises in return. They would pray for the family's dead loved ones.

This custom eventually came to the United States. It became part of Halloween. Now, children go trick-or-treating. They beg for candy treats!

People in Europe used to get soul cakes on November 2.

CHAPTER 7

The Jack-o'-Lantern

There's an Irish folktale about a man named Jack. He played tricks on the devil. After Jack died, the devil got even. He made Jack wander around at night. Jack could use only a tiny light to see where he was going. This light was a burning lump of coal. Jack carried it inside a hollowed-out turnip.

This folktale led to an Irish Halloween custom. People carved out a turnip, potato, or beet. Inside, they put a glowing lump of coal. They called it Jack's Lantern, or Jack of the Lantern. That became the word *jack-o'-lantern*!

Pumpkins are native to North and Central America. Irish immigrants discovered pumpkins in the United States. They found that pumpkins were easy to carve into jack-o'-lanterns.

Carving jack-o'-lanterns is a popular Halloween activity.

Many Irish people moved to the United States. Once there, they used big pumpkins for the lanterns.

Today, many people make jack-o'-lanterns on Halloween. They just carve a scary face on a pumpkin and put a candle inside.

CHAPTER 8

The Day of the Dead

Mexicans celebrate *Día de los Muertos* (DEE-ah day lohs MWEHR-tohs). That means "day of the dead." It falls on November 2—All Souls' Day. Both All Souls' Day and Día de los Muertos are meant to honor loved ones who have died. But Día de los Muertos celebrations begin days before November 2.

This festival fits right in with Halloween. Children wear skeleton costumes. And people eat candy shaped like skulls. They also make **altars** to the dead. They're decorated with candles, flowers, and photos. It's not a sad festival at all. It celebrates a loved one's life!

Skull-shaped candies for Día de los Muertos are called *calaveritas* (kah-lah-veh-REE-tahs). That's Spanish for "little skeletons."

Día de los Muertos is a happy time. Family and friends joyfully recall the lives of loved ones.

CHAPTER 9
Poetry Corner

FIVE LITTLE PUMPKINS

Five little pumpkins sitting on a gate.
The first one said, "Oh my, it's getting late."
The second one said, "There are witches in the air."
The third one said, "But we don't care!"
The fourth one said, "Let's run and run and run."
The fifth one said, "I'm ready for some fun!"
Woooo, went the wind
And out went the light
And the five little pumpkins rolled out of sight!

—Author unknown

THREE LITTLE WITCHES

One little, two little, three little witches,
Flying over haystacks, flying over ditches,
Slid down the moon without any hitches.
Hi-ho, Halloween's here!

One little, two little, three little witches,
Flew by a fence and tore their britches;
Had to go home and get some stitches.
Hi-ho, Halloween's here.

—*Author unknown*

TRICK OR TREAT!

Out we go
To Trick or Treat—
We don't care who we will meet.

Witches, goblins,
Ghosts in a sheet—
We're scary too, from head to feet.

Owls are hooting,
Bat wings beat—
But nothing can stop us from Trick or Treat!
Give us an apple.
That would be neat.
Or give us something really sweet.

We will share
What we get to eat,
Just so we get to go Trick or Treat!

—*Author unknown*

The Witches Song

Hoity-toity!
Hop-o'-my-thumb!
Tweedledee and Tweedledum!
All hobgoblins come to me,
Over the mountains,
over the sea:
Come in a hurry,
come in a crowd,
Flying, chattering,
shrieking loud...
Thus said a witch
on a windy night,
Then sailed on her
broomstick out of sight.
—Ruth Bedford (1882–1963)

JOINING IN THE SPIRIT OF HALLOWEEN

* Is there a pumpkin farm in your area? Visit the farm and pick out a pumpkin. Then chat with the farmers. Ask how many Halloween pumpkins they sell.

* Draw a face on your pumpkin with a magic marker. Then have an adult help you carve around the lines you have drawn.

* Is there a children's hospital in your community? Visit the children before Halloween. Bring craft materials and help them make decorations.

* Do you know a Mexican American? Ask how he or she celebrates Día de los Muertos.

MAKING SPOOKY SPIDERS

What you need:
1 cup semi-sweet chocolate chips
  or butterscotch chips
2 cups chow-mein noodles
1/2 cup pecans, peanuts, or walnut pieces

Directions
1. Place the chocolate or butterscotch chips in a small saucepan. Melt over low heat on the stove top.*
2. Stir until the liquid chocolate or butterscotch is smooth. Remove the pan from the stove top.
3. Mix in the chow-mein noodles and nuts so that they're coated in chocolate or butterscotch.
4. Lay a piece of wax paper on a baking sheet. Using a teaspoon, place about 24 small pieces of the mixture onto the baking sheet.
5. Chill in the refrigerator for about 15 minutes and then remove. Eek—your spiders have legs! Don't worry. It's just the noodles.
6. Store your tasty treats in a cool place.

*Have an adult help you operate the stove.

MAKING EGG CARTON SPIDERS

What you need:
1 paint brush
Black paint
Scissors
An egg carton
Hole punch
Black pipe cleaners
Wire cutters
Wiggle eyes
Glue

Directions
1. Have an adult help you cut the egg carton apart so that you have several little cups or sections.

2. Have an adult help you cut the pipe cleaners in half.

3. Use the hole punch to make eight holes in the bottom edge of an egg-carton section.

4. Paint the egg carton cup with black paint and let it dry.

5. Put a piece of pipe cleaner through a hole in one side of the egg carton section and out through the opposite hole. Bend the sides of the stem down. Do this three more times until you have all eight legs in place.

6. Glue on the wiggle eyes.

Now you're ready to scare up some fun. Happy Halloween!

GLOSSARY

altars (ALL-turz)—tables set up to honor someone

ancient (AUY-shunt)—from the very distant past

goddess (GOD-dess)—a female honored as a god

harvests (HAR-vests)—crops that have been gathered

immigrants (IM-uh-grunts)—people who move to another country

mischief (MISS-chef)—trouble or tricks

symbol (SIM-bull)—an object, image, or word that stands for an idea

traditional (truh-DISH-un-ull)—following long-held customs

LEARN MORE

BOOKS

Baby Professor. *Why Do We Celebrate Halloween?* Newark, DE: Baby Professor, 2017.

Beer, Julie. *Weird But True Halloween: 300 Spooky Facts to Scare You Silly.* Washington, DC: National Geographic Kids, 2020.

Elliot, Rob. *Laugh-Out-Loud Halloween Jokes.* New York, NY: Harper, 2019.

Heinrichs, Ann. *Celebrating Halloween.* Mankato, MN: The Child's World, 2022.

Marsh, Laura. *Halloween.* Washington, DC: National Geographic Kids, 2012.

WEBSITES

Visit our website for links about Halloween and other holidays:
childsworld.com/links

Note to Parents, Teachers, and Librarians: We routinely verify our Web links to make sure they are safe and active sites. So encourage your readers to check them out!

INDEX

All Hallows' Day, 10
All Hallows' Eve, 10, 12
All Souls' Day, 16, 20
All Saints' Day, 10
apples, 9, 13, 14

Black cats, 4, 15
bonfires, 6

Calaveritas, 20
candy, 4, 16, 20
Celtic people, 6, 9
Ceres (Roman goddess), 9
Christians, 11, 12, 16
costumes, 4, 6, 12, 20

Día de los Muertos, 20, 21, 26

Feralia festival, 9
"Five Little Pumpkins" poem, 22

Ghosts, 4, 12, 25
Great Britain, 6, 12

Harvest festivals, 8, 9
harvest moon, 8

Immigrants, 14, 18, 30
Ireland, 6, 12, 18–19

Jack-o'-lanterns, 4, 18, 19

Mexico, 20, 26

Nut Crack Night, 14

Poems, 4, 22, 23, 25
Pomona (Roman goddess), 9, 12
Pooky Night, 12
pumpkins, 4, 18, 19, 22, 26

Romans, 9, 14

Samhain festival, 6, 9
skeletons, 15, 20
soul cakes, 16
"souling," 16

"Three Little Witches" poem, 23
"Trick or Treat" poem, 25

Witches, 4, 12, 15, 22, 23, 25
"The Witches Song" song, 25